ADVENTURE

An Outsider's Inside View Of Getting An Entrepreneur To Market

by MOIRA VETTER

NO YO press

Published by Noyo Press, LLC.
Atlanta, Georgia, USA | noyopress.com

First Edition Print.

AdVenture.
Copyright © 2013 Moira Vetter
All rights reserved.

PUBLISHER'S CATALOGING-IN-PUBLICATION DATA

Vetter, Moira 1969 -
   AdVenture: an outsider's inside view of getting
an entrepreneur to market / Moira Vetter. — 1st ed.
   p. : ill. ; cm.
   ISBN 978-0-9885226-4-0
   1. Small business—Management. 2. Entrepreneurship.
3. Success in business. I. Title.

Printed in the United States of America.
Illustrated & Designed by Bennie Kirksey Wells.

Set in Clarendon.

adventurethebook.com

DEDICATION

I would have nothing to say if everyone I've ever known
hadn't taught me a valuable lesson. You each know what
that lesson was.

I dedicate this book to my family: Jennifer, Vivian, Leo, Mom,
Dad, Jack, Anni, Lorraine, Mike, Mom-Mom, Keely, Benie,
Auntie Donna, Uncle Tony (the EVER faithful angel), Aunt Bob
and Uncle Bell, Kim, Oliver, John, Sherry, Uncle John, Aunt
Martha, Marcy, J.P., Penelope, Aunt Myrtle, Henrietta, Loretta,
Howard, Wade and my BELOVED Modo Modo Agency family.

I further dedicate this to irreplaceable bosses and teachers
Angela Hill, Pete, Regan, Marianne, David and Michael. A special
thank you to Chris Coleman whose influence can't be quantified,
although qualifying it might make for another, very fun, book.

WITHDRAWN

There Is No Truer Adventure Than Enterprise   **7**

WIIFM   **10**

So, What Is An Entrepreneur?   **19**

Vision – The Astronaut   **27**

Passion – The Miner   **39**

Speed – The Daredevil   **49**

Risk – The Navigator   **61**

Reward – The Mountain Climber   **73**

Results – The Lion Tamer   **85**

Growth – The Body Builder   **97**

Every Ending Is A Beginning   **109**

About The Author   **117**

THERE IS NO TRUER ADVENTURE THAN ENTERPRISE.

A three year old with a briefcase at the front door who says, "I go to the office," is an entrepreneur. Because entrepreneurs are born, not made. You can make' em better...but you just can't make them.

They come pre-wired with strange ideas, fearlessness, willfulness and intoxicating energy. Qualities that are crazy, addictive and—thank God for business—often profitable.

Entrepreneurs don't look for adventure; they create it.

They don't fit neatly into the world, which is precisely why they build things to fit them. And because they are unique, they would be offended to know that they are predictable.

But they are.

Entrepreneurs and their organizations do entirely new things in entirely the same ways. And they have since the beginning of time. The guy that made fire had vision, probably struggled to contain his invention and made the others guys nuts trying to find fire's true promise and bring it to fruition.

This book is a practical guide to getting an entrepreneur to market, living through the launch of the enterprise and loving it. It is a startup manifesto, a psychology course and a go-to-market handbook that explores the seven core attributes of the entrepreneur:

1. **Vision** – How the entrepreneur sees and expresses what can't be seen
2. **Passion** – Undying desire in business and learning to love it
3. **Speed** – When to floor it and when to pump the brakes
4. **Risk** – The trade-offs for going all in or playing it safe
5. **Reward** – For some the journey isn't its own reward. Make sure they are rewarded.
6. **Results** – Framing metrics to measure not who you wanted to be, but who you need to be now
7. **Growth** – The dreamer, the thinker and the doer from startup to maturity

DON'T JUST READ THIS BOOK, USE IT. ENTREPRENEURS NEED ALL THE HELP THEY CAN GET. AND WE NEED ALL THE ENTREPRENEURS WE CAN GET.

Without them, there wouldn't be ideas, inventions or the inspiration to do the crazy things that create jobs, joy and progress.

Let the adventure begin.

(What's In It For Me?)

WIIFM

IF YOU ARE AN ENTREPRENEUR

You've got a short attention span and too much to do to read this book.

Read it anyway. The better you understand how your dominant traits impact the people that work with you, the better (and faster) you can achieve your goals. Be honest about how you are, who you work well with and what specific kinds of support you need to achieve success.

If you find in these pages patterns that feel familiar, share them with your team. If you recognize team or organizational dynamics that you aspire to, share them with your team. If you want investors, take very seriously the understanding that good ideas alone or a good idea known to no one but you is not what creates a serial entrepreneur. Investors want good ideas that can be executed, grown and sold for greater value.

(What's In It For Me?)

WIIFM

IF YOU WORK FOR AN ENTREPRENEUR

Entrepreneurs are a little crazy.

They are driven by something that sometimes only they can see. They often don't communicate in full sentences or even full thoughts. If you appreciate the passion and believe in the entrepreneur or the power of their idea, throw everything you have into it. Understand that you play a critical role in enabling an entrepreneur by bringing their vision and the business to life.

You will encounter in your career many business people and workers, but you may not encounter many true entrepreneurs. If you're bothering to read this book, you probably have one of them that you're catering to (as either a labor of love or hate).

Whatever your reasons you are smart to focus on the entrepreneur. Without these guys, there wouldn't be ideas, inventions or inspiration to do the crazy things that actually create progress, create jobs and in a great world—joy—as you see an amazing venture come to life. Thomas Edison may have been a sad story if it weren't for Charles Batchelor. Relish your role in helping create amazing things.

(What's In It For Me?)

WIIFM

IF YOU
INVEST IN
ENTREPRENEURS

Entrepreneurs are the engines of industry.

If you are an angel investor or private equity firm, you'll have different motives for investing in a venture. Some of you are interested in betting on the horse itself. Daymond John said that he puts his money on the man, because the man who has one great idea can come up with another one. Some investors, however, particularly the larger PE firms, are interested in one idea or company and not the entrepreneur at all; they may need the idea or assets for a broader portfolio objective. No matter which, this book can help you get in and get return on your investment sooner.

Regardless of your investment reasoning, there will invariably be an entrepreneur in the company you invest in. And that entrepreneur is a unique animal. You may be one and understand perfectly the mindset that drives a creator and assembler of things or people.

What is most important, and what this book can help with, is understanding how important and diverse the teams around the entrepreneur are and how they change in different settings. You will see the attributes identified in your entrepreneurs. You will likely see the dynamics described and the challenges they pose for the teams that surround them. This book can help with much more than understanding the situation, but understanding is the first key to making progress.

You want a return. You will get
that return faster if you are able
to assess not only the value of
the current entrepreneur, brand,
team and company...but also the
challenges and timeline you've set
aside for transforming the asset
(the man or the machine) into what
you want it to be. The quicker you
can find partners who understand
not only your goals, but what must
happen to achieve success given the
dynamics of the organism in your
hands, the sooner you can realize
that valuation and earn your return.

This book can help you see what DNA exists in your entrepreneur and the challenges they are facing based on organizational dynamics so you can help them be more effective. While every investment and every entrepreneur is special—as the old saying goes,

"EVERYONE AND NO ONE IS SPECIAL."

History does repeat itself and many of the patterns described in this book can help you quickly identify challenges, the potential path to success and the partners you need to help you achieve it.

SO, WHAT IS AN ENTREPRENEUR?

People hear the word entrepreneur all the
time. But what is he? Or she? *

An entrepreneur is so much
more than somebody that starts
a business. They seize upon an
idea and marshal the resources
to make it real. They are much
more than business people—
they are forces of nature.

Entrepreneurs, particularly the "serial" kind, are risk
takers. They are creators and builders. And they never stop
moving, building, doing, growing and starting over again.

* We're not gonna play that male/female game here where we swap pronouns.
  We'll say he because it's shorter.

ONWARD & UPWARD.

Entrepreneurs exist in every environment and hold a variety of job titles. Not every CEO is an entrepreneur and not every entrepreneur is well-funded or within sight of their goal.

ENTREPRENEURS ARE PEOPLE DRIVEN BY VISION & POSSIBILITY.

These unique creatures sometimes need collaborators who can work with them regarding their vision and the creative side of their interests. This may prevent an entrepreneur from feeling alone and enhance their pleasure in exploring the possibilities of an idea.

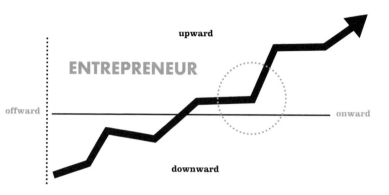

Other times, entrepreneurs need partners who can help actualize their ideas through planning, prototyping, building, testing or espousing their value. Believers that are trained properly, and equipped with the proper DNA, naturally live on both sides of this line—one moment a visionary or visualizer and the next a master executor.

THE MARRIAGE OF AN ENTREPRENEUR TO THEIR PARTNERS IS FRUITFUL WHEN INSTINCT & PLANNING ENSURE UPWARD MOMENTUM.

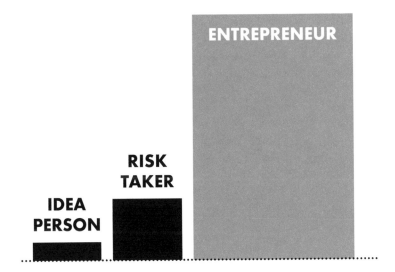

An entrepreneur possesses a unique combination of attributes and perspectives that drive them perpetually forward and upward. There are basically two kinds of entrepreneurs—replicative and innovative. Both types are self-motivated and hard-working but come at their pursuits from different perspectives.

"Replicative entrepreneurs" are the guys that create and repeat stable money-making businesses, often franchise organizations. They follow a repeatable, structured formula and apply discipline to run their businesses. They are creative risk-takers with their capital, but often take an existing, proven model to scale, create jobs and repeat their successes.

"Innovative entrepreneurs" spark new ideas that go far beyond the creation of jobs and business models. They can seem at once inspired and disruptive. They are often relentless charmers—and are responsible for the creation of categories and entire industries.

Study either type of entrepreneur and you will see a familiar set of seven characteristics or attributes at play during different phases of their ventures. Picture your current job or business and see which of the following is most influencing your current success or struggle on the way to greatness.

THE SEVEN ATTRIBUTES OF ENTREPRENEURS.

Which of these attributes have you seen an entrepreneur project along the way to fueling industry and job growth? Consider your role in the venture and consider how each of these seven aspects controls or enables you.

VISION

HITCH YOUR WAGON TO A **STAR.**

Ralph Waldo Emerson

ALL PROGRESS BEGINS & ENDS WITH VISION.

The entrepreneur has a gift for vision.

A special kind of vision that enables them to see what may not be visible. Things that are so far away or so different from the shape of what exists that others cannot see them.

(And perhaps something that doesn't yet exist.)

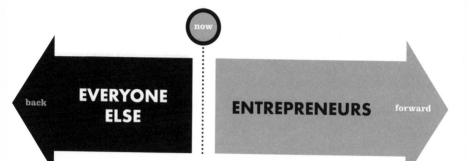

ENTREPRENEURS ARE FORWARD-THINKING

and have an exceptional ability to navigate through moving, shifting objects and environments, undergo intense speeds and anticipate complex trajectories in their path toward a defined endpoint.

The wise entrepreneur is steadfast in his commitment to his vision. He understands his vision is far more than a destination.

Vision is what defines the undertaking in its entirety. It is what reinforces the mission from inception through barriers, through doubt, through competitive challenges, through change and finally, upon arrival, to a spectacular and somehow familiar reality.

EVERYTHING CHANGES. VISION TRANSCENDS CHANGE.

Along the way, vision is what fuels, steers and guides.

The function of the entrepreneur's vision changes from launch to mission completion.

One moment, vision sets the entrepreneur apart, gives him focus in defining what the venture will be and in charting the course from Point A to Point B. In the next, vision is the gravitational pull that holds the enterprise together, drawing like-minded people into the system and ensuring all elements are working in tandem toward a common goal.

Moving through the mission—from launch to flight to landing—the entrepreneur experiences different realities, and is subject to varying elemental forces. Training and experience have readied the entrepreneur to be constantly vigilant to these shifts in atmosphere, and to adapt to those changes.

VISION HELPS STEER THE COURSE THROUGH CHANGE, EVEN WHEN THE FOCUS OF THE MISSION BECOMES OBSCURED.

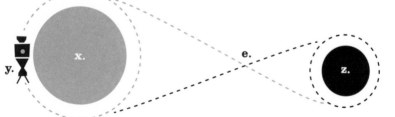

x. - where you started
y. - you

z. - where you're going
e. - everything that can change

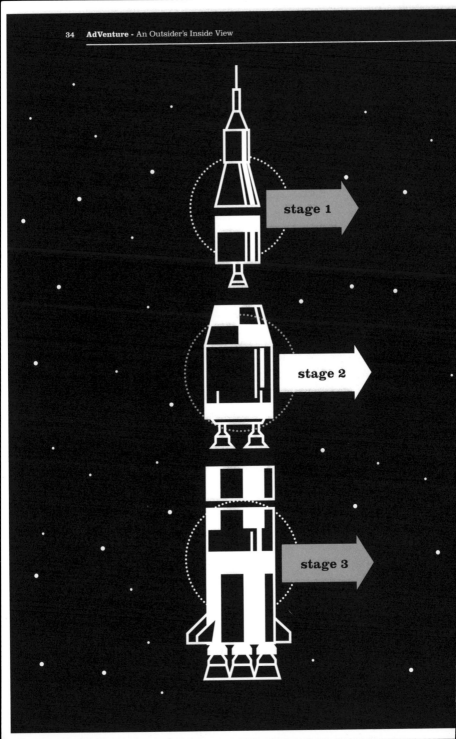

FROM RADICAL INNOVATION TO MAINSTREAM ACCEPTANCE.

Even as the venture evolves, the entrepreneur relies on vision through every stage of the mission.

Stage 1 - Launch

It takes guts to be among the first to set foot on a new planet. Unknowns abound and risk is high. The frontier itself poses significant challenges. Launching this sort of mission requires complete confidence in one's vision and faith that it is achievable. The vision is a rush of adrenaline that propels the venture past inertia and into orbit.

Stage 2 - Exploration

Once the frontier has been crossed, the unknown decreases and the known increases. There may be less turbulence at cruising altitude, but vision must still be actively engaged. Experimentation becomes more likely, and more challenging, as greater numbers participate.

Stage 3 - Landing

Vision ensures a safe landing at the intended destination. This stage may be different than imagined, daunting or even come too soon. With each safe landing the likelihood of future missions and greater daring increases.

VISION
CHOOSE YOUR OWN ADVENTURE: *

* In life, you can always choose the role you play. Today you may work for the entrepreneur, tomorrow you may be the entrepreneur, next week you may be the investor. Your adventure is ALWAYS yours to choose.

VISION - IF YOU ARE THE ENTREPRENEUR

There are things that only you can see. Things that only you can conceive of in your mind's eye. Do not keep your treasure trapped there. It is your duty as an entrepreneur, in fact it is your disease, to get those ideas out, onto a napkin, into the public domain, out where they can do good, do harm, do anything. What is it that only you can see?

VISION - IF YOU WORK FOR THE ENTREPRENEUR

If the person that owns and runs the company you work for doesn't have a vision they have shared, ask them what it is. If they tell you they don't know, you have a serious problem. If they tell you, but you don't understand them, ask more questions. Chances are you are not the only one that is unclear on the vision. If you understand the vision but don't see what's so exciting about it, ask the entrepreneur why it excited them...or better yet...why it excites your customers. For you to make a contribution and play a part in making a difference you must know where you're going, why you're going and truly care about getting there. What is the vision of the company you work for?

VISION - IF YOU INVEST IN THE ENTREPRENEUR

If you get excited about a visionary entrepreneur or a singular business idea sparked by an entrepreneur...grab it. But make sure you are clear with the entrepreneur about the role you may play in shaping, growing, altering, or maybe even killing that vision. Investors' motives are as endless as the stars in the galaxy. To keep an entrepreneur in league with you, to protect or transform the person or the idea, it is critical that they understand where their vision ends, your vision begins and whether the two can and will come together. There can only be one vision. Who controls the vision in this venture?

DIG
DEEP.

TRUE ENTREPRENEURS HAVE PALPABLE, UNSTOPPABLE PASSION.

It is a force as indescribable and illogical as faith—and as undeniable. Entrepreneurs draw on passion constantly, instinctively and reflexively to drive them.

Entrepreneurs bring an energy, an alchemy, that is otherwise missing. Passionate entrepreneurs feel untapped potential and are driven to isolate and bring it to light. To do, to create, to be, to pursue, to explore. That is their passion.

It is what drives entrepreneurs past the point where others stop. They smell the vein of gold or the oil a few inches away. It could be unmined potential or ideas in themselves. It could be someone else's raw talent or visionary idea. Those with authentic desire are unstoppable because they simply must have what they feel and know to be priceless.

They don't call them "divining rods" for no reason. **Passion is drawn to the divine.**

WHEN WORK, COMMITMENT & PLEASURE ALL BECOME ONE & YOU REACH THAT DEEP WELL WHERE PASSION LIVES, NOTHING IS IMPOSSIBLE.

Nancy Coey

BURNING DESIRE.

Napoleon Hill asserted that "definiteness of purpose backed by a burning desire" is essential to success. Driving passion can transform the will of one person into magic by finding the market, the product, the promised land, the cure, the secret formula or the inner strength to succeed.

The entrepreneur sometimes has no interest in execution. Talk of logistics or capitalizing an effort are things that happen somewhere else in the brain. Or perhaps in someone else's brain. That is where partners and investors may be needed the most.

While others may be controlled by their logic or cling to the security of safe ground, the entrepreneur has a desire to dig deep. Look at the ventures that have successfully launched with paltry resources, flawed execution, questionable timing or an unclear growth path. Sometimes, passion is the only thing that gets you to market—in spite of all other facts and forces.

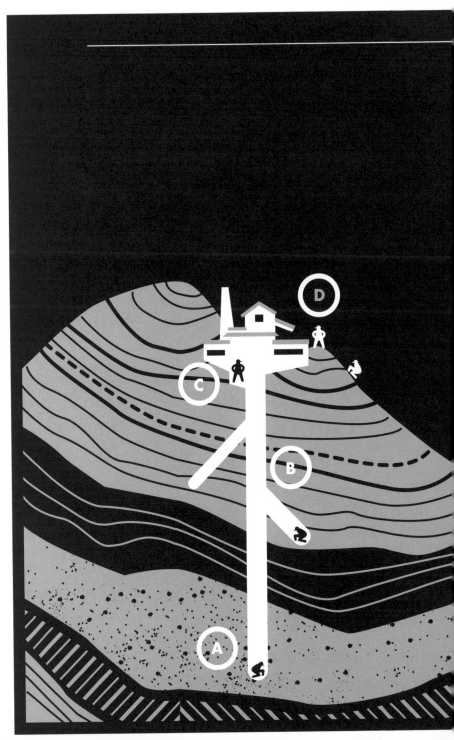

EXCAVATING EXHILARATION

ENTREPRENEURIAL TEAMS & PASSION.

Passion frees the entrepreneur from the constraints of reason and inspires limited resources to dig deep, take risks and yield rapid success.

A. Passion drives the entrepreneur to the core despite the fact that no one has yet opened up this path

B. Pursuit leads to the depths of risk and reward, and demands brave allies and partners

C. Strategy may appear erratic, but is actually the result of expert plotting

D. Some stakeholders are apprehensive and may even walk away because they can't yet see what the entrepreneur passionately believes in

PASSION
CHOOSE
YOUR OWN
ADVENTURE: *

....

* In life, you can always choose the role you play. Today you may work
  for the entrepreneur, tomorrow you may be the entrepreneur, next week
  you may be the investor. Your adventure is ALWAYS yours to choose.

PASSION - IF YOU ARE THE ENTREPRENEUR

There are times in the launching of a business, a brand, or a concept where an entrepreneur can feel utterly alone. At these times, when forces seem against you, when you fear the light at the end of the tunnel may be a train, you must call on your passion. Others may not understand you or the well from which you continue to draw your belief. Passion, the most primal of the assets you have for getting to market, is a reserve that must be preserved at all costs. You must love the pursuit with all your heart and soul.

PASSION - IF YOU WORK FOR THE ENTREPRENEUR

See the passion in the entrepreneur's eyes and draw your inspiration from it. Entrepreneurs need you to believe in them and share their passion even if you don't completely understand it. Organizational passion, also known as morale, is widely recognized as key to the health of a culture. Similarly, you must value and protect the entrepreneur's passion, because it is as powerful, as tangible and even more essential to health and survival than morale. Love what you do.

PASSION - IF YOU INVEST IN THE ENTREPRENEUR

No sound investor should put money on an entrepreneur who does not exhibit mad passion for what they do. The critical thing for an investor is to ensure that passion is met with sound ideas, willing teams and actual progress toward the goal. Entrepreneurs may survive on passion alone, but you shouldn't put your money on the guy that brings nothing but passion to the table. You just may have to love them and leave them.

SPEED

A NEED FOR SPEED.

Speed is key to every decision and action an entrepreneur makes, but speed is relative. Hitting a ramp isn't about going the fastest you can, but controlling your speed and knowing when to pick up the pace.

TOO FAST,
you overshoot your landing.

TOO SLOW,
you eat it in the buses.

It's all about control, pace and preparation.

In business, as with Evel Knievel's famed Snake River Canyon jump, people usually only remember the official take-off and landing. But long before the fateful launch, work goes in to studying the terrain, testing the idea, measuring the strength of the launch vehicle, coordinating the efforts of the launch crew and more.

THEY ONLY REMEMBER THE LANDING ANYWAY.

S

An entrepreneur that goes too slow is likely one who can stomach the risk of starting, but who allows fear or disorganization to interfere with acceleration through the moment of truth.

An entrepreneur that goes too fast and overshoots a landing is often someone who has thoroughly baked and delivered an offering before a community is ready for it. Many entrepreneurs worry about missing a market window that is closing—but not about the considerable risk of smacking into a wall before the window has opened.

The entrepreneur that gets the timing and speed just right is an inspiration. Of course, they probably won't sit still long enough to discuss their good fortune because they are already at work on their next venture.

People typically remember the official take-off and landing while the entrepreneur is focused on the process and the climb.

THE SUCCESS OF THE JUMP IS SIMPLY A MOMENT IN TIME

for the entrepreneur who sees the landing zone but is already pacing himself for the next big leap.

AN ENTREPRENEUR THAT
GOES TOO FAST

and overshoots a landing is someone who has a delicious, thoroughly baked offering before a community is ready for it. The cost of over-shooting a landing to the entrepreneur can be wasted resources for unnecessary heroics or landing where the cameras and the crowds can't witness the glory. Rapid launches should be tested with an open mind for modification: Which attributes will be embraced by the most people? Which features are missing that would drastically spike demand? Moving the fastest is only a positive attribute when the entrepreneur is equally willing to be the fastest in altering their course if the market asks.

AN ENTREPRENEUR THAT
GOES TOO SLOW

is likely one whose tolerance for risk gets the better of them at the moment of truth. A businessperson may move along at a good clip and need to quickly scale his or her organization or offering. Stalling at a critical moment where speed would give the momentum to span a divide or push past a barrier is a fate many organizations have met. They may cap their growth for comfort or simply because the organization does not understand how to change to sustain the speed and flexibility the smaller organization leveraged to gain their early advantage. Choking back at this time may stop the entrepreneur on the ramp or land him in the buses.

AN ENTREPRENEUR THAT
GETS THE SPEED JUST RIGHT

is an inspiration. Of course, they probably won't sit still long enough to discuss their good fortune because they are already at work on their next venture. As we said about the audience or the market, while they typically remember the official take-off and landing, the entrepreneur is focused on the process and the climb. The success of the jump is simply a moment in time for the entrepreneur who sees the landing zone and is already pacing themselves for the next big leap.

FASTER
FASTER.

Moving fast is a competitive advantage.

It is essential to all fast movers and bleeding edge enthusiasts to be the first. However, being first with an idea and being first with a business model and proposition that maximizes market opportunity are very different things.

TIME TO MARKET
VARIES WIDELY DEPENDING ON THE INDUSTRY.

In technology, ideas can be brought to fruition and launched in 60 or 90 days and completely played out in the mass market within 12 to 16 months. For a rocket scientist, an aggressive timeline might look like 5 to 10 years from conception to launch, and 10+ years before the product (which will never reach a mass market) is obsolete.

Entrepreneurs, and those that help them achieve their goals, understand the relative importance of speed and work to help the business shave off enough time to safely or responsibly actualize an idea and beat the competition.

THE BENEFITS OF SPEED:

- Income gains from NOT missing out on revenue opportunities. Some call this "time to revenue" or "speed of return"

- Market share gains from establishing early leadership in an area

- Reduced time-to-market for a new delivery platform that can transform delivery of all offerings

- Reduced cost-to-produce by locking in enough early market share to negotiate better sourcing costs

Many consulting organizations, associations and academic institutions study time-to-market to quantify it. Time-to-market should not be viewed as a theoretical concept because it has a real-life impact on both the top line and the bottom line.

Here is one statistic on the value of speed in time-to-market:

For a pharmaceutical company with annual revenues of $2 to $10 billion per drug, "time is money" carries real meaning. Cutting time-to-market by a single week for a major drug can mean a difference of up to $200 million in revenues.

How much does shaving one week off your product launch cycle earn you?

CALCULATE YOUR RETURN FROM ACCELERATION:

	EXAMPLE	YOUR FIRM
Annual Revenue (company-wide or by product)	$10,000,000	
Divide by 52 Weeks	$10M / 52 = $192.3k	
Best Case: Potential earnings per week if this is your only offering	$192k per week	
Realistic Case: Assume the offering only represents 10% of your potential revenue	$19k per week*	

* Weigh these potential revenue losses the next time you assess a proposal from an outsourced partner or overtime/bonus expenses for your own employees to accelerate a launch.

SPEED
CHOOSE
YOUR OWN
ADVENTURE: *

* In life, you can always choose the role you play. Today you may work for the entrepreneur, tomorrow you may be the entrepreneur, next week you may be the investor. Your adventure is ALWAYS yours to choose.

SPEED - IF YOU ARE
THE ENTREPRENEUR

You probably aren't afraid of moving fast. In fact,
you probably love it. Just remember, you not only
need to move fast, you may need to change fast...
or stop on a dime. You may work with others that see
you as a blur. If you're going to floor it, balance your
need for speed with your market and your team.

SPEED - IF YOU WORK FOR
THE ENTREPRENEUR

Some people are drawn to entrepreneurs and their ventures
because speed looks fun. Some people think moving fast
will get them instant gratification or get them "rich quick."
If you are supporting an entrepreneur, be prepared to move
faster than you may be comfortable, and know that fast
change is inevitable, but don't think you're getting *out* of
anything fast. Most people don't get rich quick. They try
and fail and sometimes succeed with speed. That "getting
rich" part isn't covered in this chapter because it usually
happens slowly and methodically...often as a direct result
of your efforts, support and staying power.

SPEED - IF YOU INVEST IN
THE ENTREPRENEUR

As an investor, you have to be clear about what you
want in return for your capital and how soon you want it.
You also have to remember that a fast-moving entrepreneur
can't get you faster return on your investment if the
market isn't ready. Constantly revisit the exit date you
want for a liquidation event or the velocity of return
you expect. If you are a long-term player, find a fast-
moving entrepreneur with a long-term view so they don't
run out of roadway before your investment pays off.

RISK

RAISE THE
ANCHOR.

When an entrepreneur builds a business plan and maps a course, many factors affect the direction they take. Often the entrepreneur is innovating in an area where others haven't been.

Some call this finding a "blue ocean."

Anyone charting a course knows that blue oceans don't stay blue for long. They become red with the blood of the feeding masses. Entrepreneurs do not seek blue oceans because they are calm; they seek them because they have not been claimed. Like a blue ocean, any environment surrounding an entrepreneur does not stay still or calm for long, either.

An entrepreneur hopes to navigate to the greatest reward with the least risk. He is a very risk tolerant individual because he knows risk offers dividends.

After all,

NOTHING VENTURED,
NOTHING GAINED.

SOMETIMES THE ONLY WAY AROUND IS THROUGH. *

*Looking at this image is reminiscent of Winston Churchill's
fantastic quote: "If you're going through hell...keep going."

WHY AND WHEN THE ENTREPRENEUR GOES AROUND (INSTEAD OF THROUGH)

Making the way gradually, while observing market leaders & testing premises
Research and development, and BETA stages of growth, offer a rare and often fleeting opportunity to observe and test a business idea. This can be done along the periphery, while studying market leaders and the markets the entrepreneur wishes to serve.

Avoiding struggling industries & avoiding being positioned among the competition
In some industries the top two or three companies are like crabs in a bucket, drawing each other back in, away from escape or progress. Going around the traditional players and making a way to the new world is a way to avoid or resist the baggage, damage or destruction that could occur by going through.

Leapfrogging a current market or offering
Skipping the trip through the current environment is a fast and high-risk journey. The entrepreneur in this scenario formulates a course to go around or go over rapidly.

WHY AND WHEN THE ENTREPRENEUR GOES THROUGH (INSTEAD OF AROUND)

A richer journey comes from experiencing the barriers & bumps of the direct route
Some of the best business people, and consequently the best marketers, have seen the risky terrain and the ugly terrain up close and personal. It provides context and credibility.

Plowing on through also builds character and creates rich stories that generate emotion and appeal to our humanity. Those are the things that resonate and make us appreciate our accomplishments.

The fastest way from here to there is through the middle
It takes time to go around obstacles, time that entrepreneurs often do not have. Although it can be daunting and dangerous, sometimes putting an offering out in the market and pushing it forward quickly is the best way.

WHEN WE LOOK BACK ON OUR LIVES, WE REGRET THE THINGS WE DIDN'T DO MORE THAN THE THINGS WE DID.

THINGS YOU DIDN'T DO

1%

THINGS YOU DID

99%

The percentage of regret for the things you did and did not do in your life.

When looking at industries that offer the potential for huge gains, they are usually rife with risk.

It's not essential to win all of the time...just ENOUGH of the time.

Calculating risk and playing the odds enable entrepreneurs to take chances where others wouldn't. Winning enough of the time is what helps fund the often unavoidable miscalculations that come with launching a new venture.

WHAT DOES CALCULATED RISK LOOK LIKE?

EVERYTHING IS A RISK TO SOMEBODY	ENTREPRENEURIAL ENVIRONMENT (FAST, LOOSE)	NON-ENTREPRENEURIAL ENVIRONMENT (SLOW, TIGHT)
Confronting a competitive threat directly	Do so with passion and belief. If you're going to get on the soapbox, crow loudly about why you're a better choice but then ENSURE you deliver immediately.	Take the high road by getting closer to the customer and confronting the issue one-on-one where it matters.
Ignoring a competitive threat	While you're ignoring the threat, quickly create one of your own by leveraging a strength that trumps the competition.	If you choose to ignore a threat, be sure to engage someone in research about the issue. Be sure you are ignoring the right things and not the things that matter most to your customers.
Launching several things at one time	It's one thing to get the balls in the air. Once they are there, just be sure you have the right people in place to KEEP the balls in the air and manage the growth.	Be clear in the organization about who is responsible for each aspect of each launch. If you are structured and hierarchical, you may get people to take more risks by creating healthy competition.
Launching one thing at a time	There's a risk of becoming bored unless you are madly in love with your single product or service or cause. Avoid risk by staying engaged or continually reinventing your primary invention.	This is a huge risk because a group that is risk averse has all their money riding on one horse. There is a reason that Win-Show-Place tickets are popular...you don't have to pick one.

RISK/REWARD ANALYSIS FOR ACTING

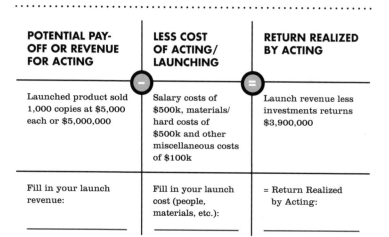

POTENTIAL PAY-OFF OR REVENUE FOR ACTING	LESS COST OF ACTING/LAUNCHING	RETURN REALIZED BY ACTING
Launched product sold 1,000 copies at $5,000 each or $5,000,000	Salary costs of $500k, materials/hard costs of $500k and other miscellaneous costs of $100k	Launch revenue less investments returns $3,900,000
Fill in your launch revenue:	Fill in your launch cost (people, materials, etc.):	= Return Realized by Acting:
_____	_____	_____

RISK/REWARD ANALYSIS FOR NOT ACTING (OPPORTUNITY COST)

POTENTIAL LOSS OF REVENUE FOR NOT ACTING	AMOUNT SAVED OR NOT SPENT BY NOT ACTING/LAUNCHING	LOST OPPORTUNITY COST*
		* This cost may be compounded if a competitor acted when you didn't. Then your lost opportunity cost is accentuated by their opportunity gain.
Assume lost revenue of -$5,000,000	Saved investment of $1,100,000.	Cash to spend elsewhere is $1.1M. Lost Opportunity here is $3,900,000. If the company could not raise the $1.1M, the lost opportunity is irrelevant. However, if the company does not invest in opportunity A in order to invest in opportunity B with greater revenue or a lower investment cost then there may in fact be no loss, but rather a more significant gain.
Fill in your potential lost revenue:	Fill in your saved investment	= Lost Opportunity Cost:
_____	_____	_____

RISK
CHOOSE YOUR OWN ADVENTURE: *

* In life, you can always choose the role you play. Today you may work for the entrepreneur, tomorrow you may be the entrepreneur, next week you may be the investor. Your adventure is ALWAYS yours to choose.

RISK - IF YOU ARE
THE ENTREPRENEUR

Risk can be exciting but it must be measured and calculated.
Are you risking your own funds or someone else's?
Don't burn a future capital bridge you may need. Are you
risking your reputation? You may never get that back.
Most other risks are acceptable and essential to success.
Just be honest about what you stand to gain and make
sure your other vested partners understand whether
you are betting the farm or just this year's crop.

RISK - IF YOU WORK FOR
THE ENTREPRENEUR

It is sometimes easier to tolerate risk when you support
an entrepreneur because it isn't your money, your dream
or your future in play. Relish your role as someone
who can challenge whether a risk is worthwhile with
some objectivity. Understand that your diligence,
communication, research and management can help
mitigate risks as a venture moves to market.

RISK - IF YOU INVEST IN
THE ENTREPRENEUR

You wouldn't be an investor if you didn't have a tolerance
for risk. But you first and foremost have a desire for gain.
You know that by withholding capital you can stop an
entrepreneur and avoid a risk. But investment is not
typically about withholding, it's about how to make your
money work. Finding the type of entrepreneur whose
risk tolerance maps to your own can provide you with
a hell of a lot more fun when investing than simply
logging onto a website and buying shares of a fund
whose classification aligns with your "risk profile."

REWARD

THE
CLIMB
IS ITS
OWN
REWARD.

Reward manifests itself in many shapes and forms at every phase on an entrepreneur's climb to success: at the beginning, in mid-ascent, at the summit and in preparation for the next quest.

For those that climb, rewards come not only from reaching the peak, but from the very decision to climb, from applying their capabilities and from their determination to succeed where others have not ventured.

Entrepreneurs come wired for the climb and understand reward is not a static endpoint.

IT IS A PROCESS OF DEFINING THE JOURNEY AND ACHIEVING VICTORIES EVERY DAY.

A RANGE OF REWARDS

EMOTIONAL, FINANCIAL & INTELLECTUAL

It's always about the next great conquest.

IN THE BEGINNING STAGES of climbing toward an objective, rewards emerge from recruiting the right team, obtaining investment capital and recognizing you have the right tools for the climb.

IN THE MIDDLE STAGES of ascent there is both a sense of accomplishment and a sense of anticipation. The entrepreneur benefits from the perspective of where he has been and focuses strategically on where the journey leads next. Mid-climb, the entrepreneur's reward emerges from using the experience of the early climb, drawing on the skills and synergy of the core team, and leveraging the new position of higher ground to exploit coming opportunities.

AT THE END OF A CLIMB, arriving at the summit is in many respects its own reward. For the entrepreneur it is a reward with some exclusivity because so few arrive—less than half survive into their fifth year. Survival and arriving at the first summit are short-lived and little incentive for the entrepreneur. The end is inevitably another beginning, with greater potential and future prospects for loftier heights and even more fruitful or harder won rewards.

m.

b.

LIKE A JOURNEY, BUILDING A REWARDING VENTURE IS A PROCESS.

Entrepreneurs need to hone their business instincts, discipline and communication skills to organize and succeed in the climb. They learn that their communication needs and challenges—both internally and externally—change as the climb strategy shifts and as the rewards themselves change.

Companies in the early stages of foundation-building must establish **awareness** so people understand who they are. Next, comes the need to build **credibility** in an effort to be recognized as a serious, qualified business. Then companies must establish their offering's direct (and differentiated) **value** to their target audience. Lastly, the company must inspire **action** to buy or engage them repeatedly.

It is sometimes difficult, but absolutely critical, for an entrepreneur to understand the rewards that different stakeholders seek as a venture moves through its life cycles. The journey itself may be the payoff for the entrepreneur, but all the other stakeholders—the ones needed to get to the summit—may have their sights set on more tangible, continuous rewards. Add the complexity of generational differences in rewards theory, and an entrepreneur can no longer sprint to the top with an adoring, "dues-paying" crowd. Everyone needs to understand direction, feel valued, understand and achieve in their role, remain flexible and see that success is possible.

STAGES OF THE CLIMB	CHALLENGE AT THIS STAGE	REWARDS OF EXITING THIS STAGE
Awareness	**Internal:** Lack of understanding of goal/destination **External:** Lack of awareness of the vision or possibility	Completing the basic awareness stage is a huge triumph in building a foundation. It offers clarity for quickly moving through the next stages.
Credibility	**Internal:** Lack of faith, frequent questioning or resistance **External:** People drawn to obvious leaders or trusted users if you don't have credibility	Completing this stage enables you to stop talking about yourself and focus your energy, your solutions and your vision on the external party.
Value	**Internal:** Team unable to express value from the external perspective. What is the external party's reward? **External:** Inability to see or believe compelling value. What is my clear reward?	Completing this stage helps you define a framework of value and differentiation that can guide the rest of the climb and all future ascent strategies. This enables the entrepreneur to spread the vision further and faster... and through other people's words and actions.
Decision Action Belief Loyalty Recommitment	**Internal:** Not all believers are prepared for the final ascent or conditioned to make the journey. **External:** Not all initial buyers are the best match for sustained or profitable growth.	Completing this stage enables the entrepreneur to harness the enthusiasm and belief of others to propel the climb. The entrepreneur can modify and diversify the ascent strategy for impact—and focus on replicating it.

Serial Entrepreneurs develop formulas or processes for taking an idea or organization from inception to the peak. As they reach one summit and look ahead to the next, they seek to apply what they have learned from their last climb when undertaking their next quest. They seek to be smarter and better, and repeat only the things that contributed to the return and reward in the first climb.

Consistently building strength and allegiances when acquiring capital, building a core team and creating business growth tools are all fundamental to repeatable success. Reward comes not only from knowing what to do, but from knowing what to say and do—again and again.

Strategy and tactics must be run in tandem:
- Outline strategic and tactical initiatives and steps
- Run them in tandem where there are no dependencies
- **Result:** Weeks or months are shaved off the launch cycle

Rapid prototyping of the business case:
- Determine the decision-maker (consensus will not be sought until the external market drives it)
- Establish a quick baseline of objectives
- Provide many, varied prototypes to gain early feedback
- Refine business concepts and proposed rewards quickly
- **Result:** The business is shaped by the gut of the buyer or key stakeholder. The serial entrepreneur understands that having his thumbprint on the idea is not essential and is useless if there is no interested market.

REWARD
CHOOSE YOUR OWN ADVENTURE: *

---

* In life, you can always choose the role you play. Today you may work
for the entrepreneur, tomorrow you may be the entrepreneur, next week
you may be the investor. Your adventure is ALWAYS yours to choose.

REWARD - IF YOU ARE
THE ENTREPRENEUR

You are likely preconditioned to enjoy each stage of your climb. You will likely be as motivated by failures as wins. But to be successful as a serial entrepreneur, and to be seen as a true leader or visionary, your model for growth must ensure that rewards are shared by those wired differently than you...time after time.

REWARD - IF YOU WORK FOR
THE ENTREPRENEUR

Everyday working for an entrepreneur isn't always rewarding. They can be demanding people. But to be successful in an entrepreneurial environment, you must be fascinated and fed by your place in the Petri dish. You live the experiment and contribute to growth every day. If your experience isn't rewarding, change your contribution or work with the entrepreneur to redefine a more satisfying short-term and long-term role for you. Know that there is a growth formula, know where you fit and figure out if you've got what it takes to do this again and again.

REWARD - IF YOU INVEST IN
THE ENTREPRENEUR

Financial gains may seem like the logical reward for an investor. In fact, many investors take a much deeper interest in their investments. People underestimate the passion, interest, care, flexibility and pleasure that investors gain from making someone else's climb possible. If your sole reward will be money, look away often enough to give the entrepreneur space. If you're in it for adventure, get in the game, be at the table and enjoy the climb with the team. And, if you have a dream that involves combining two entrepreneurial ventures into one, give the leaders an early warning about your vision so neither climber loses motivation or altitude.

RESULTS

START
WITH
THE END
IN MIND.

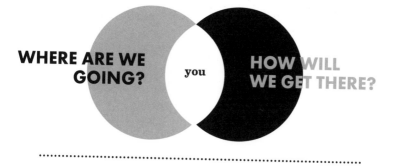

Attaining the desired organizational results is achieved by asking two questions:

WHERE ARE WE GOING? HOW WILL WE GET THERE?

The entrepreneur begins his journey by identifying the desired direction, then diligently focusing on progress, understanding the risks and nurturing the company toward the end result.

The most challenging part of being a results-oriented organization is having the foresight to align all aspects of the business toward the end game. Knowing the stages of growth means that the company can be nurtured through every phase with active intent, ultimately leading to the results that management predicted and planned for.

When we aspire to make a successful result second nature, we must first train and practice diligence on the way to accomplishment and we must tame the things that might deter us from our end goal.

TRAIN YOUR BUSINESS TO ACHIEVE RESULTS THROUGH EVOLVING DISCOURSE.

At every stage of organizational growth, the successful entrepreneur recognizes changes in developmental focus, shifts in risk and differing approaches to incentivizing progress.

a. **In the beginning,** the entrepreneur focuses on the form that the business will take—defining the goals and results that will guide the organization to success. This stage lays the foundation for future success. It is key to start out in the right direction with a clear statement of expectations.

b. **Next comes a period of testing relationships** and establishing power dynamics. To reach the desired future results, rising above conflict and challenges is par for the course. The internal structure as well as the external proposition should and will be tested. Effective communication moves the company efficiently though this phase.

c. **As the company becomes more established,** it defines norms of the roles and processes that make things work. In this phase, the company builds toward increasingly predictable results, balancing the inherent risks of doing business with the potential gains of market wins and efficient growth.

d. **Entering maturity,** the organization becomes focused on how it performs and where it can still realize growth. Even as the organization moves from one successful result to the next, it must continue to redefine the arena and the rules of play to ensure greater results.

e. **Ultimately, you will transform the organization.** Having fulfilled its original potential, the venture will fine-tune operations to prepare for a new life cycle. Results in this phase can take the form of achieving new growth through product innovation, differentiation, by exploring new markets or by exiting a market or industry entirely.

RESULTS
MEAN
DIFFERENT
THINGS
in different
organizations

METRICS

THE METRIC	SAMPLE MEASUREMENTS
Brand Measurement	Brand valuation, size, ranking in comparison to competitors.
Client Satisfaction & Expansion Measurement	Client retention rates, expanded client revenue, percentage of new market growth.
Awareness & Exposure Measurement	Numbers of viewers or listeners, impressions and amount of engagement.
Profitability Measurement for Different Customer Sets	Customer profitability by type, by industry, by product, etc.
Market Share Measurement	Market size and percentage of sales by category, industry, etc.

ORGANIZATION TYPE

MEASURING RESULTS IN AN ENTREPRENEURIAL ORGANIZATION	MEASURING RESULTS IN A NON-ENTREPRENEURIAL ORGANIZATION
Brand equity is often intangible. The entrepreneurial organization may be more comfortable with this and might realize non-traditional measures of brand value. There may, however, be challenges in tracking and building consistent value.	While this type of organization may struggle with something seemingly intangible, the non-entrepreneurial organization is more likely to be diligent about measuring strengths against competitors and developing tools for continuously measuring results.
Entrepreneurial organizations are more comfortable trying new methods and approaches for attaining and retaining customers. On the flip side, they may have difficulty staying the course if customers want to keep what they already have rather than trying something new.	With more delineated structure, this organization may not ask as many creative questions, or explore new ways to achieve client satisfaction. This group benefits from diligence of tracking and consistency of delivery.
Entrepreneurial organizations often seek less traditional measures of reaching audiences, like social media, loyalty initiatives and less quantifiable signs of evangelism. Don't forget to tie engagement metrics to those that buy.	Traditional measures may be familiar and readily available from media outlets and existing statistics. Just as the entrepreneurial organization, ensure data is being compared to direct sales data.
The entrepreneurial organization fluidly shifts focus to zones of success, including higher performing clients and trendy segments. The latest target markets and marketing media aren't always the most profitable, but the tolerance for risk based on the promise of a future reward can lead to larger long-term results.	It may be easier in a non-entrepreneurial organization to get information about performance by segment or offering. But there is also resistance to getting rid of less profitable clients in order to focus on more profitable opportunities. There may also be a refusal to accept that a once high performance segment or industry is no longer profitable or deserving of the primary focus or investment.
An entrepreneurial organization may commit to any opportunity that presents itself and fail to focus on an existing market foothold. Failing to penetrate existing markets, looks in the short-term like "money left on the table," but the greater loss is actually failing to achieve market leadership which enables future expansion.	The non-entrepreneurial organization benefits from maximizing their share in existing markets, but may miss opportunities in expanding or "emerging" markets.

**LONG-TERM RESULTS CALL
FOR PATIENCE AND JUDGMENT.**

THERE IS A TIME
FOR RESTRAINED
PROFESSIONALISM,

AND A TIME FOR THE FLOURISH OF EXPERTISE.

RESULTS
CHOOSE
YOUR OWN
ADVENTURE: *

* In life, you can always choose the role you play. Today you may work
  for the entrepreneur, tomorrow you may be the entrepreneur, next week
  you may be the investor. Your adventure is ALWAYS yours to choose.

RESULTS - IF YOU ARE THE ENTREPRENEUR

As an entrepreneur it is critical to remember that your final end-game is not the "key" result. Steady progress is the key result you will be measured on. You must learn to discipline yourself to achieve the measured results at each stage that will continue to win the confidence of the customer, the team and the investor.

RESULTS - IF YOU WORK FOR THE ENTREPRENEUR

Many people with vision and charisma lack a detailed nature or the ability to focus consistently on key results. If you can become the ally that knows the growth path and can hold the organization (if not the entrepreneur) accountable for achieving results, you may be the magic pixie dust that assures success. Nearly every great brand and business success story has both a well-publicized entrepreneur and a tireless, talented execution agent without whom success would have remained on a napkin, in a plan or in the hopeful mumblings of some really smart people. Make measuring and reporting results your job. Don't wait to asked.

RESULTS - IF YOU INVEST IN THE ENTREPRENEUR

Perhaps here in the area of results, more than any other area, is where the clarity of an investor can assist an entrepreneur. It is the very disciplined consistency and contextual long-range view that are characteristic in an investor, and sometimes absent in an entrepreneur, that are necessary for all stakeholders to win with the venture. While investors have put in, and stand to gain, much more than capital, often the reasoned discourse regarding funding is the greatest gift you can give an entrepreneur.

GROWTH

SUSTAINED GROWTH IS THE UPSHOT OF PLANNING PREPARATION & PACING

Growth is neither about incessant consumption, nor random acquisition. Successful growth takes strategic preparation, sound planning and controlled pacing.

When a company is poised for success, it may seem that the only initiatives that make sense are those that point toward increasing staffing or the size and scope of operations. But how should these strides be made? Is growth always appropriate? And if not, when should an organization seek other ways to succeed?

PLUMP UP... OR PERISH!

It is often said that "if you're not growing, then you're dying." This type of approach is an oversimplification. What's most important is preparation, pacing and adjusting to the challenges of growth at each stage of the company's life.

Many books are written about business owners' decisions to 'stay small' or fix their growth. As long as margins continue to grow, this can sustain a business owner for a period of time. However, this is most likely the approach of a business owner looking to draw cash out of a business rather than to grow value and sell the business. For a buyer to take sufficient interest—particularly a private equity group or set of professional investors—the business likely needs to show top line and bottom line growth. It's OK to pause for sanity, to reconsider a market, to recapitalize, or to correct a move, but in short order...a true entrepreneur will set the business back on an upward top and bottom line trajectory.

CALCULATED GROWTH LEADS TO STRATEGIC CONQUESTS, WHICH LEADS TO MEASURED MATURITY.

Being geared for growth is about staying one step ahead—of yourself. If your only thoughts fit who you are now, it's time to 'size-forward' and start thinking thoughts appropriate to who you'll soon be.

Understand what is required at different phases of business growth.

Seed to Startup
From Startup, the wise entrepreneur understands the importance of overcoming the challenges of market acceptance, and finding niche opportunities. Growth is a natural result of the early phases of the business lifecycle. In Startup you must use energy on planning, matching your offerings to opportunities, defining your business structure, calculating a profitable revenue model and charting an organizational vision you can grow with.

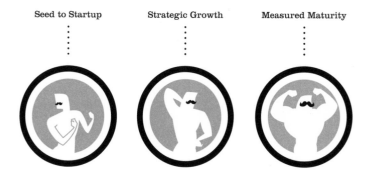

Seed to Startup   Strategic Growth   Measured Maturity

Strategic Growth

When a company is established and growth becomes a reliable
constant, effective management will seek to optimize outcomes.
These performance goals may be increasing sales, expanding
into new markets and opening new distribution channels.
Adjustments must be made to accommodate continued growth:
perhaps a revised vision, new channel partners, additional
employees or a new roadmap entirely.

Measured Maturity

It's also important to plan for when the business reaches
maturity, hits a plateau or experiences a decline and it is
time to exit. Changes in market conditions transform mature
industries overnight. Opportunities may have materialized
due to someone seeing a strategic advantage in acquiring
your business. The savvy entrepreneur is always open to
these prospects and is ready to hear out interested parties
and consider the exit opportunity.

Throughout every phase, there is a need for continuous
assessment and action: What form should growth take in our
next phase? How does our growth path align with our mission,
vision and industry trends? How should we communicate these
shifts internally and externally? Where do these choices leave
the entrepreneur, the organization and the investors?

ALL CHANGE IS NOT GROWTH

AS ALL MOVEMENT IS NOT FORWARD.

Ellen Glasgow

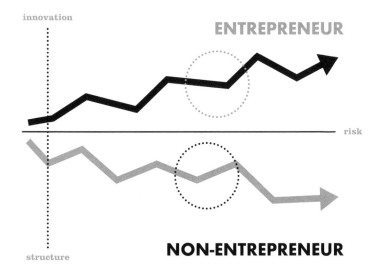

innovation

ENTREPRENEUR

risk

NON-ENTREPRENEUR

structure

ORGANIZATIONAL DYNAMICS WITH ENTREPRENEURS & NON-ENTREPRENEURS

Growth inspires different actions in different environments. Here is a contrasting look at how growth affects entrepreneurial and non-entrepreneurial organizations differently. Even if individuals are pro-growth, the culture of an organization will shape how well teams keep pace.

THE CHALLENGES PRESENTED BY GROWTH

ENTREPRENEURIAL ORGANIZATION	NON-ENTREPRENEURIAL ORGANIZATION
Challenge: Introducing structure and infrastructure. **Management struggles to find time to create this structure, particularly when they're busy inventing and delivering.**	Challenge: Staying profitable. **It's easy to load on infrastructure but difficult to maintain the lean/leverage you had before growth turned to expanded overhead and sometimes bloat.**
Challenge: Adapting to new structure and infrastructure strategies. **"Why can't we do it the way we used to?" Because you're not that organization anymore.**	Challenge: Taking the risks that growth brings with it. **Managers may not want to endanger newfound success which sometimes stifles further growth. Continued risk-taking is often paralyzing for a technician-driven organization.**
Challenge: Focusing on new business growth to the exclusion of growing existing accounts. **This can begin to negatively impact profitability because existing accounts, who deliver recurring and often increasingly greater margins, are not being nurtured or expanded.**	Challenge: Focusing on organic growth to the exclusion of new business growth. **It is second nature to take care of existing business, but failing to target new accounts actually increases the risk of dependency on a few key accounts. Diversify, diversify, diversify.**
Challenge: Not finding talent fast enough. **When you hit a growth curve or an uptick in a market, not having talent inhibits your ability to respond to opportunities. If speed is the key, outsourcing or partnering may be the best bet.**	Challenge: Failing to identify the most profitable accounts and retire the least profitable accounts. **Your least profitable accounts take as much or more time to manage as your most profitable ones. Underperforming clients limit your growth by sapping resources. Cutting these accounts may seem counter-intuitive when the goal is growth.**
Challenge: Not finding money fast enough. **Money doesn't grow on trees. It takes structure, discipline, good references and a solid plan to convince an investor.**	Challenge: Spending money on both conservative and risky propositions. **A diversified approach to investments, R&D, channel partner pilot programs and other types of opportunity tests ensures that you succeed while mitigating risk.**

GROWTH
CHOOSE
YOUR OWN
ADVENTURE: *

* In life, you can always choose the role you play. Today you may work
for the entrepreneur, tomorrow you may be the entrepreneur, next week
you may be the investor. Your adventure is ALWAYS yours to choose.

GROWTH - IF YOU ARE
THE ENTREPRENEUR

There are few things more exciting than growth.
It is important not to get caught up in the ego of
higher revenues, fancier offices or an impressive
headcount addition. Growth is only about those
things as far as the benefit to the organization they
deliver. Prepare yourself now for the changes you
will need to make in yourself and your approach
in order to successfully grow your company.

GROWTH - IF YOU WORK FOR
THE ENTREPRENEUR

During periods of heavy growth the entrepreneur
desperately needs you to be their eyes and ears. They will
operate on auto-pilot and may be unaware of changing
dynamics, changing morale, changing functional
requirements, etc. Growth is truly a team effort and
in this area more than any, you will be needed for
your resources, instincts, potential employee referrals,
willingness to do more and fearlessness in the face of
change. Thinking big is one thing, getting big will
count on you in more ways than you can imagine.

GROWTH - IF YOU INVEST IN
THE ENTREPRENEUR

All entrepreneurs think they need more money, more
people and more space to successfully grow. Make them
prove it to you. There are many things that can be done
with nothing. There are times when fewer people being
more productive is optimal. Make sure you know when
to force efficiency and when to go all in to help a venture
accelerate its growth.

ALWAYS BEGIN WITH THE END IN MIND.

Beginnings are about a clear vision, a north star of possibility and a passion for what may seem impossible to many. Thank heavens entrepreneurs are rarely stopped by others' definitions of possible or reasonable. That's why entrepreneurs are such powerful forces for progress and why they are so essential at this time. At any time. And that impossible, improbable thinker or tinkerer needs people that believe in him. This is timeless. One of the best Henry Ford quotes is, "I am looking for a lot of men who have an infinite capacity to not know what can't be done." People with vision and passion always find those believers.

Getting believers behind an idea is kind of the easy part because now the urgency of market opportunity demands speed and execution. Everybody likes to joke about the incongruous grouping of "fast, cheap and accurate," proclaiming "pick two!" Most people won't settle for only two—and entrepreneurs in fast growth mode typically don't have the luxury of delivering just two and hoping to scale. Not unless they've got an investment partner that believes the vision, accepts the need for both speed and accuracy, and is willing to supplement the cost differential to allow for rapid growth.

It is these kinds of "pick two" trade offs in the heat of execution or in the absence of capital that introduce risk—with real consequences—into the enterprise. Reputations are on the line. Personal and business assets are at stake. Group morale and customer satisfaction are under a microscope and risk finds an interesting way of shifting around and scaring everybody involved.

Some people find this risk culture unsettling while others find it exhilarating. Entrepreneurs typically come wired to handle risk but their teams may be hanging on by their fingernails. The investor could start putting the screws to the operation if risk doesn't appear reasonably calculated or monitored. Sometimes survival in this edgy environment is possible by focusing on the rewards of the journey and of the creation.

A REMINDER OF THE GOAL CAN GIVE THE TEAM STRENGTH AS THE PRESSURE FOR RESULTS GETS HARDER.

Sometimes this is the time where the entrepreneur starts dreaming of new pursuits and imagining new beginnings while others take on the necessary discipline of delivering repeatable results and growth.

And as linear as all this sounds, there is rarely a smooth transition from stage to stage. There are fits, stops and starts. The entrepreneur and the team are torn backward and forward as the business matures. It is in this battle for sustainable growth that communication and the core team's chemistry will enable success or drift into decay. Commit to team building and clarity of purpose because decay during fast growth is nasty—and it takes way longer to recover from than it ever took to create.

Just as you will wear different hats during your career, a business also has many incarnations and restarts throughout its life. And rarely with the same group of people, depending on how "exciting" the growth turned out to be. Ultimately, the entire journey, the company, the invention— exemplify the transformative reality that is growth. No one can take back the experience of the one who imagined the idea, the ones who supported and executed on that vision, and the ones who paid for the privilege of the experiment. The experience and the AdVenture of enterprise is magical because it transforms the players—through the process of creation—into accomplished, stronger, new people. How powerful is that?

HOW WONDERFUL TO BE AT THE END OF AN ADVENTURE... AND TO BE ENTIRELY NEW.

Alive with new visions, new passions and new possibilities. Because the people that make the future know you should always finish what you start. And you must always end with a powerful new beginning in mind.

ABOUT THE AUTHOR

Moira Vetter didn't get serious about business until the second grade. That's when she started running the register in her father's pharmacy and got a first hand look at the rise and fall of an entrepreneurial venture.

Today she is the founder and CEO of Modo Modo Agency, an award-winning, business-to-business marketing firm that has won over 100 awards in its first 5 years. Modo Modo Agency, Moira's second entrepreneurial venture, won the #2 spot in the Atlanta Business Chronicle's 2010 Fastest Growing Women-Owned Firms ranking. The firm has offices in Atlanta and Los Angeles.

Moira began her professional career 25 years ago on the client side in technology and healthcare before moving to the agency world, working in several well-known national firms.

In her career she has helped more than 170 businesses with well over 200 products and services define, launch, grow and even divest of their ventures.

She serves on the Executive Advisory Board and is Past President of the Atlanta Chapter of the America Marketing Association. She sits on the board of the Oxford Center for Entrepreneurs and is a member of the Leadership Atlanta Class of 2013. Moira also serves on the Georgia Department of Education's Marketing Cluster to help develop marketing curriculum for Georgia High School students. She was a featured Entrepreneur in the 30th Annual Consortium for Entrepreneurship Education, was a featured speaker at the Nonprofit Leadership Alliance and is a guest entrepreneurship blogger for Frazier & Deeter. She has appeared on Fox News, CBS Atlanta and CNBC.

Moira commits the resources of Modo Modo Agency to a variety
of non-profit efforts and service projects. With her DoGooder
program, she quarterly closes Modo Modo Agency for a full
day and takes the staff off-site to serve their chosen charity.
In 2012 the company helped MedShare, The Study Hall, The
Foundation for Hospital Art and the Dunwoody Nature Center.
In the past, DoGooders have done service for Open Hand Atlanta,
the American Cancer Society Hope Lodge, The Center for
Self-Sufficiency/Café 458, Uplift Internationale, the Global
Soap Project, homestretch and Books for Africa.

In addition to volunteer service, Moira's company donates
significant pro bono professional services to other firms.
In 2012 alone they supported Great Promise Partnership, SWEA
Southwire Engineering Academy, Georgia Watch, Oxford Center
for Entrepreneurship, OnBoard (formerly Board of Directors
Network) and Wear Your Soul Foundation. Past organizations
served include 12ForLife, Ecole du Samedi and HireOne Atlanta.

**Moira is a sucker for a good
cause and an even bigger sucker
for entrepreneurial charmers.
She hopes that this book will draw
even more of them into her sphere.**